Chinese
MYTHOLOGY

Other titles in the *World Mythology* series include:

Chinese
MYTHOLOGY

Don Nardo

ReferencePoint
Press®

San Diego, CA

© 2021 ReferencePoint Press, Inc.
Printed in the United States

For more information, contact:
ReferencePoint Press, Inc.
PO Box 27779
San Diego, CA 92198
www.ReferencePointPress.com

LIBRARY OF CONGRESS CATALOGING-IN-PUBLICATION DATA

Names: Nardo, Don, 1947- author.
Title: Chinese mythology / by Don Nardo.
Description: San Diego, CA : ReferencePoint Press, 2020. | Series: World
  mythology | Includes bibliographical references and index.
Identifiers: LCCN 2019054035 (print) | LCCN 2019054036 (ebook) | ISBN
  9781682828090 (library binding) | ISBN 9781682828106 (ebook)
Subjects: LCSH: Mythology, Chinese.
Classification: LCC BL1825 .N37 2020 (print) | LCC BL1825 (ebook) | DDC
  299.5/1113--dc23
LC record available at https://lccn.loc.gov/2019054035
LC ebook record available at https://lccn.loc.gov/2019054036

CONTENTS

HIERARCHY OF ANCIENT CHINA'S BEST-KNOWN GODS

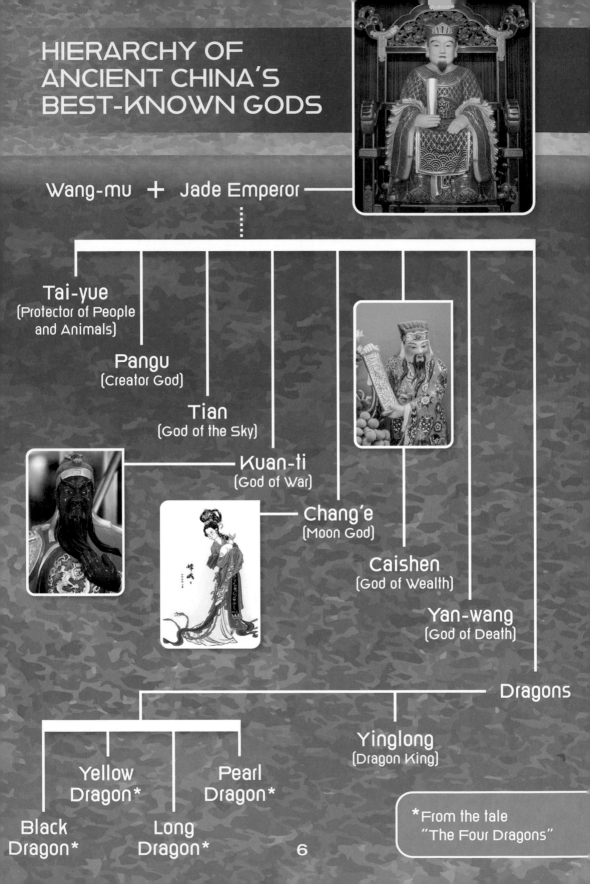

Wang-mu ✛ Jade Emperor

Tai-yue
(Protector of People
and Animals)

Pangu
(Creator God)

Tian
(God of the Sky)

Kuan-ti
(God of War)

Chang'e
(Moon God)

Caishen
(God of Wealth)

Yan-wang
(God of Death)

Dragons

Yinglong
(Dragon King)

**Yellow
Dragon***

**Pearl
Dragon***

**Black
Dragon***

**Long
Dragon***

6

*From the tale
"The Four Dragons"

A Fascination with Spirits and Monsters

Long, long ago, in a remote region of China, there lived a farmer who over time accumulated an immense amount of hay. Indeed, his haystack eventually grew to the size of a small mountain. The farmer paid little attention to his haystack until one day when he noticed an elderly man standing near it. A few days later he saw the strange man again. After spotting the old man several times, the farmer finally walked over and asked him if he needed some assistance.

The elderly man replied that no assistance was necessary. The reason he had been hanging around the haystack, he explained, was that he had recently taken up residence in it. Sure enough, the man showed the farmer an apartment consisting of several rooms, which he had hollowed out of the hay. The elderly fellow politely invited the farmer to stay for some tea. The farmer agreed, and they spent the afternoon having a pleasant conversation about a wide range of subjects.

No Ordinary Old Man?

In the weeks that followed, the farmer visited the old man in the haystack several more times. During that time, the farmer also noticed that the man went away early each morning and returned a few hours later. When questioned about it, the old man explained that he often had breakfast with a friend who lived on the other side of China. That was impossible, the farmer said, for no one could cover that great distance so quickly. At that moment the farmer became both suspicious and wary. He said to himself that either the old man was lying or something more sinister might be at work.

Before the farmer could give the matter any more thought, the old man invited him to accompany him to the distant breakfast he had spoken of. Reluctantly, the farmer said yes, at which point the man grasped his arm, and in a flash the two of them rose up high into the air. Shocked and disoriented, the farmer looked down and saw fields, rivers, forests, and mountains whizzing by far below. Surely, he thought, this was no ordinary old man; rather, he must be a supernatural being of some kind. The question was whether he was a beneficial god, like Shen-nong, the deity who protected farmers, or an evil spirit, perhaps one of the Mogwai, horrible demons who hunted human prey.

> **SHEN-NONG**
> The god who taught humans agriculture and protected farmers

The farmer soon had his answer. The flying duo suddenly dropped out of the sky and landed, unharmed, in a town the farmer did not recognize. Moreover, the elderly man, who was still holding the farmer's arm, no longer had human form but was revealed to be a fox. There were said to be a few good foxes, the farmer recalled. However, rumor had it that most foxes were deceitful or downright wicked, in which case the farmer might now be in serious trouble.

> **MOGWAI**
> Evil demons who sought to harm humans

At that instant, the fox led the farmer into a nearby restaurant, where the manager served them a fine breakfast. Perhaps, the farmer reasoned, this was one of the good foxes. After all, he claimed that each day he had breakfast in a far-away town, and that was indeed what had just transpired. Unfortunately for the farmer, however, that happy thought proved to be misguided. The fox smiled, bade the farmer goodbye, and abruptly disappeared into thin air. The farmer now found, to his dismay, that the fox had marooned him in a strange town more than one thousand miles from his farm. Only through the kindness of some local residents, who sympathized with his plight, did he manage to borrow enough money to cover his travel expenses back home.

Spiteful, Nasty, or Otherwise Malicious

The tale of the farmer who had been fooled by a fox was a myth told and retold in China for many centuries. It was not the only story involving foxes in the Chinese corpus, or collection, of myths, for foxes appear in those stories more often than any other animal.

Foxes appear in Chinese myths more often than any other animal. The majority of foxes in those tales are mischievous or mean spirited and frequently play pranks on humans.

Furthermore, just as the farmer himself surmised, helpful foxes were exceedingly rare. Most foxes were either badly behaved or downright evil and enjoyed playing mean-spirited pranks on humans.

As for why foxes had such negative images and personalities in ancient China, no one knows for sure. But modern experts think it was because they were strongly associated with death and dead people. From the earliest times foxes, who often feast on carrion, or the bodies of dead animals, were frequently seen climbing out of people's graves or coffins. So they gained a reputation for being the wandering souls of deceased humans. In turn, they were closely associated with ghosts and spirits.

Mostly these ghosts were spiteful, nasty, or otherwise malicious, and some were out-and-out monsters who ate human flesh. Thus, the farmer with the big haystack was fortunate that the fox he encountered only wanted to badly inconvenience him. Also, as happened in the farmer's tale, foxes typically transformed themselves into sympathetic characters, especially old men and attractive young women, in order to get closer to their prey.

Such stories of mischievous or monstrous foxes are so strongly embedded in Chinese society and lore that even today those creatures' images are widely viewed as scary. As a result, when Chinese children dress up as ghosts and other monsters in Halloween-type celebrations, many choose to portray foxes. This fascination for spirits and monsters, which has become a genuine national craze, stems directly from China's hefty collection of ancient myths. "The ancient Chinese took ghosts very seriously," Chinese educator Sara Lynn Hua explains. "Western monsters are fairly well known across the globe," she continues. "You have zombies, werewolves, vampires, dragons, etc." In China, in comparison, she says, "you have an array of different, yet equally terrifying, demons and apparitions. From ancient times, the Chinese have created stories of demons and monsters to explain the things that go bump in the night."[1]

CHAPTER ONE

The Ancient Chinese and Their Gods

China maintains a cultural tradition rich in ancient folklore and myths that are populated by gods and other supernatural beings. That is not surprising, considering how long Chinese civilization has existed. The country was the site of one of the four so-called cradles of human civilization. (The other three were in Egypt; India; and Mesopotamia, now Iraq.)

The initial Chinese culture arose in the mid- to late 2000s BCE along the banks of the Yellow River, in northeastern China. At first there were no large cities or kingdoms. Rather, most people dwelled in small farming villages erected on or beside the fertile soils the river had laid down over time in its wide valley. The gods these people worshipped and the myths surrounding them, if any, remain largely unclear.

The first advanced civilization in China—featuring kingdoms ruled by emperors and their governments—appeared circa 1600 BCE and over time spread to China's other river valleys. Experts divide Chinese history thereafter into eras called dynasties. Each dynasty consisted of the reigns of a series of rulers from the same family line.

The first dynasty—the Shang (ca. 1600–1050 BCE)—was centered in the Yellow River's valley. The Shang era witnessed the introduction of a number of social customs and religious rituals that were destined to carry on throughout the rest of China's ancient history. That included collecting and retelling whatever myths then existed. Initially, however, and for many centuries to come, those retellings and the perpetuation of myths was done by word of mouth. Although a writing system emerged around 1200 BCE, in Shang times it was not used to record religious ceremonies or myths.

The first written versions of China's myths appeared close to one thousand years later. Some of those written stories are undoubtedly based on tales from the long preceding oral tradition and are therefore very ancient. But other written myths arose over time, so Chinese mythology consists of a complex mix of older and newer tales. Also, writers in different parts of China frequently recorded their own personal variations of widely popular myths. As a result, University of Cambridge scholar Anne Birrell points out, "Chinese myth survives in numerous versions, the content of which is broadly consistent, but which shows significant variation in details."[2]

Minor Local Gods

That theme of variation in beliefs and myths was also applied to the Chinese gods and their identities, roles, and relative importance to humans. Over the centuries separate pockets of civilization grew up in scattered areas of China, including several river valleys, the mountains, the seacoasts, and so forth. Parts or all of them were sometimes united by one ruler or dynasty, yet the local areas long retained many of their individual customs and beliefs. That included their local gods. As a result, no overall pantheon, or group of related gods, was ever completely accepted by everyone, even when certain rulers promoted one. Certain crucial or colorful deities were more or less accepted in a majority of regions. But often they went by different names in different areas, and with a few

ZAO-SHEN
The minor deity of the kitchen who monitored a family's behavior and reported to a higher god

The congenial kitchen god Zao-shen (pictured) was thought to oversee people's homes and bring prosperity and good fortune to deserving families.

notable exceptions, most gods were not related to one another by marriage or parentage.

Among the hundreds of separate members of this complex collection of gods were what might be called minor local spirits. These included household deities who supposedly protected the home. There was a guardian of the front door, for example, and a protector of the bedchambers. Another local god oversaw the lives of wives and mothers in their homes, and still another helped husbands and fathers succeed in their professions.

The most important of these household gods was the kitchen god, Zao-shen. He did much more than just oversee the kitchen itself, as explained by historical researcher Emily Mark:

> Zao-shen was responsible for the happiness of the home and the prosperity of the family, but this depended on their behavior and values. Every month Zao-shen left the home to report to the local gods and spirits on the family's conduct. If they had behaved well, he was instructed to increase their riches and happiness; if they had behaved badly, he was told to withdraw riches and happiness. "Riches" meant not only material wealth but comfort and well-being, which was further assured by his warding off evil spirits.[3]

Civilization's Overseers

More universal and powerful were a number of gods who oversaw large aspects of human civilization and its institutions. Yan-di, for instance, oversaw fire and its many uses by people; Yan-wang was the god of death and the afterlife; Caishen was the deity of wealth; Guan-yin was the goddess of mercy and compassion; Kuan-ti was in charge of war; Tian held up the sky; and Yue Lao was the god of love.

KUAN-TI
The god of war

Yue Lao's most famous myth was also one of the favorite folktales told by the ancient Chinese. One evening a man named Wei Gu noticed an old man reading a book by the light of the moon. Wei did not realize that the old man was the love deity Yue Lao. When Wei asked the old man what he was reading, the answer

Statues like this one, depicting Yue Lao, the god of love, stand in a number of town squares across China. In his chief myth, he kept a book containing lists of future marriage partners.

was a long list of who was going to marry whom in the near and far future. Thinking the old man was insane, Wei scoffed, but the old man insisted he was telling the truth and said that Wei himself was in the book. Pointing at a little girl walking with her father, the old man said that the girl was none other than Wei's future wife. To show how little he believed the old man, Wei pulled out a knife, stabbed the girl in the back, and ran away.

Fifteen years later, Wei finally decided to get married. After he had searched for a wife for months, a government official offered Wei his daughter's hand. The official said he was anxious to find her a husband because a number of possible suitors had rejected her. When Wei asked why, the official said that she walked with a limp because fifteen years before someone had stabbed her in the back. At that moment, Wei realized that the old man he had met in the moonlight years before was Yue Lao and had been telling the truth. Soon afterward, Wei married the young woman,

YUE LAO
The god of love

15

and she turned out to be a loving wife, so he was relieved that he had not killed her.

Chinese artists most often depicted Yue Lao as a kindly looking elderly man. But many of the other gods were portrayed as looking like animals or a mixture of human and animal. Also, several deities were regularly portrayed in paintings and statues in the company of various animal companions. Common animal features among the gods, according to Birrell, included

> serpentine tails, tiger fangs, bovine [cow] horns, and avian wings, which are emblems respectively of fertility, ferocity, aggression, and aerial flight. Queen Mother of the West [Wang-mu] is represented with wild hair, the fangs of a tigress, and a panther's tail. Three bluebirds bring her food. In the later [artistic] tradition, she is accompanied by a nine-tailed fox and guarded by a leopard. Many deities are represented with snakes in their ears and riding dragons through the sky.[4]

Deification and the Jade Emperor

Another factor that complicated the identities and images of the ancient Chinese gods was the fact that some of them did not start out as divine, immortal beings. Rather, they were initially ordinary humans who, because of their extraordinary achievements, were deified, or made into gods. Usually, officials in individual ancient Chinese governments made the decision to deify someone. But to make it look legitimate to the people and country as a whole, they claimed that the so-called Queen of Heaven, the goddess Wang-mu, had chosen the candidates and actually made them divine.

Sometimes the deified person ended up as a sort of honorary sacred being having little actual power or divinity. This was the case with Guan Yu, a warrior who lived in China's Three Kingdoms period (220–280 CE). He became so famous for his courageous military exploits that he was deified.

The Supreme Deity

Shang-ti, more often called the Jade Emperor, was the supreme deity of Chinese worship and mythology. (He went by many other names as well, including Yu-di and Yu Huang Shang-ti.) In early Chinese history, well before he took on his emperor-like image and status, he was a powerful sky god who bore different names in different parts of the country. Over time, he assumed an increasing number of important duties, including overseer of law and order, justice, and in some places even creation. He was also credited with controlling the weather, regulating the passage of the seasons, and teaching humans the fundamentals of architecture. At some point, new myths were assigned to him, including the major one that claimed he had started out as a human hero and had been deified, thereby becoming a divine entity.

Rituals of worship naturally developed around the Jade Emperor. One observed his birthday on the ninth day of the year's first lunar month, when Taoist temples held special rituals appropriately called "heaven worship." It included people prostrating themselves (lying facedown on the floor or ground), burning incense, and making offerings. These consisted of several types of food, among them fruits and vegetables, noodles, cake, and wine.

Other times, however, a deified person rose to high status in the heavenly realm. This was the case with the Shang-ti, better known as the Jade Emperor. Several myths, some of them with conflicting content, tell of his human origins, the most common of which pictures him as an ordinary mortal who lived thousands of years before the emergence of the first dynasty. Very well meaning, the story went, he desired to aid his fellow humans and did many good deeds. But over time he became sad that he could not stop everyone's suffering. So he retreated to a remote cave in the mountains and there underwent hundreds of personal moral trials. Eventually, aided by some unnamed gods, he emerged from the mountains as a powerful divine being. In fact, thereafter known as the Jade Emperor, he long remained the leader of the Chinese gods.

This and the other tales about how the Jade Emperor came to be were manufactured by various dynastic Chinese rulers who sought to provide him with a mythology of his own. That helped cement his place as the chief god. By picturing him as an emperor with a heavenly court of divine officials, mirroring the earthly courts of human emperors, those rulers legitimized and solidified their own system of rule.

A Unique Blended Religious System

Whether perpetuating old myths or inventing new ones, rulers and government officials had to work within the religious system that existed in ancient China. That system of beliefs and rituals grew more complex and mature over time. It began, back before the Shang era, as a fairly simple folk religion, which modern experts often call ancient China's "popular" faith. The system of worship it featured consisted of praying to various gods, as well as noteworthy human ancestors, and making offerings of food to them either at grave sites or at small shrines set up in most homes. On the community level, meanwhile, people held annual festivals honoring the gods.

Yet that situation changed, because over time three new belief systems entered China—Taoism, Confucianism, and Buddhism. Each had a profound effect on the way the gods were perceived and on the formation of the myths associated with them. Interestingly, rather than compete against one another, these systems actually complemented one another, as well as the older folk religion. All four systems blended and produced a unique outlook on life and faith in which the gods became *less* important as objects of worship and *more* important as examples of how people should live their lives. The blended system strongly emphasized proper, productive behavior, honesty, and caring for one's fellow human beings. That new outlook altered people's views of the gods and their mythology, so some older myths changed or were replaced by newer ones.

This process is well illustrated by the effects of Taoism in the years following its appearance in China in the 500s and 400s BCE.

That belief system was built on the concept of people living in harmony, not only with other people but also with the universe's natural flow of events. That is, Taoists sought to avoid willful behavior that disrupted the normal, tranquil order of life. They tried instead to be unselfish and to put the greater good of the community over the individual person's selfish desires. Since the normal order of life in those days featured kingdoms ruled by kings and emperors with complex government administrations, it seemed only right to picture the gods and their mythical lives as mirroring the "natural" earthly system. It was Taoism, therefore, that most promoted the myths of the Jade Emperor and his heavenly court advisers.

A modern drawing depicts the fifth-century BCE Chinese philosopher Confucius, who advocated that people should maintain high ethical standards and always try to do the right thing. His ideas are reflected in many myths.

The Evolution of Wang-mu

When Taoism, Confucianism, and Buddhism entered China, each caused small to moderate changes in the images of existing gods and the myths associated with those deities. One divine being who underwent a particularly eventful evolution in both physical image and duties was the Queen of Heaven (also referred to as the Queen Mother of the West), Wang-mu. During the early Chinese dynasties, she was a local goddess worshipped mainly in the country's western sector. Then called Xiwang-mu, she was animalistic and vulgar, and artists depicted her with a panther's tail, tiger's teeth, and wild hair. According to Chinese scholar Lihui Yang, she was the goddess of "punishment, calamity, and disease." One of her specialties was "roaring and she wore a jade *sheng* on her head. Many Chinese scholars interpret *sheng* to be a hair ornament, but some argue that wearing a *sheng* meant cutting off the animal's hide and wearing it."

Later, Yang continues, toward the end of the Han dynasty (206 BCE–220 CE), her "image changed greatly from a wild and ferocious monster-like deity to a cultivated queen." Now more often called Wang-mu, she became a graceful goddess who was extremely interested in ensuring that human beings were happy. Modern experts believe this major change in her demeanor and role was the result of Taoist influences. The Taoists also helped shape the image of the chief god, the Jade Emperor, and during the initial centuries of Chinese Taoism, a myth depicting Wang-mu marrying the Jade Emperor appeared.

Lihui Yang et al., *Handbook of Chinese Mythology*. New York: Oxford University Press, 2005, pp. 218–19.

Confucianism and Buddhism

In a similar manner, Confucianism put its own spin on Chinese mythology. Begun by the Chinese philosopher Confucius (ca. 551–479 BCE), this system took hold in China in the century following his passing. It advocates morality, ethical standards, and proper behavior for both individuals and governmental systems. Confucius taught that the gods should be respected as moral examples for humans and that the latter should strive to be good, pious, humane, and honest. Confucianism encouraged the worship of the traditional gods. Also, in the same way that Taoism did, it constructed or perpetuated myths about the gods with story lines that encouraged conservative family values and ethical, responsible government.

Ethical behavior, both on earth and in heaven, was also a major pillar of the third new belief system—Buddhism, which began to spread in earnest in China in the first century CE. The Buddhists, who followed the teachings of Indian spiritual leader Gautama Buddha (ca. 563–480 BCE), held that unhappiness is caused by suffering and that suffering can be overcome by practicing ethical behavior, proper speech and actions, kindness, honesty, and following the golden rule (treat others as you want to be treated).

Buddhism placed less emphasis on emulating or pleasing the gods and more on acting ethically simply because it is more humane and constructive than acting in ways that cause suffering. Nevertheless, Buddhists accepted the existence of divine beings. Also, within China's increasingly complex belief system, Buddhism primarily promoted deities and their myths that adhered to its principles. Thus, most of the myths about the goddess of mercy and compassion, Guan-yin, were introduced by Buddhist

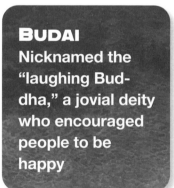

BUDAI
Nicknamed the "laughing Buddha," a jovial deity who encouraged people to be happy

leaders. They also introduced a new god named Budai. A deified version of a real tenth-century-BCE Chinese holy man, as a deity he had a jolly nature and promoted happiness. Because artists always depicted him smiling or laughing, he gained the nickname of the "laughing Buddha."

All of these blended belief systems supported an overall concept of how China should be ruled and how the rulers could ensure the country's prosperity by maintaining a healthy relationship with the gods. That concept became known as the

Heavenly Mandate. The noted English scholar of world religions John Bowker explains it, saying,

> If the ruler was just and he carried out sacrifices to heaven and worshiped the ancestors, then cosmic, natural, and human order would be maintained, and the ruler would retain the Heavenly Mandate. If the ruler neglected his ritual duties and moral responsibility to the people, then social and natural disorder would follow, and the Heavenly Mandate would be withdrawn. Rebellion would then occur and a new ruler would emerge.[5]

Diverse aspects of this interplay between humans on earth and the gods on high run through a large proportion of Chinese myths, many of which remain highly entertaining to members of each succeeding generation.

CHAPTER TWO

Creation of the World, Humans, and Culture

Most of the world's national mythologies deal with two principal aspects of creation—that of the gods and universe, and that of human beings. One way in which Chinese mythology is different from most others is that the ancient Chinese felt that a third kind of creation was important enough to describe in myths. It was the beginning of culture. Or put another way, it was the start of advanced civilization, as opposed to the ages in which people were savage and lacked agriculture, organized religion, and the arts. As Chinese scholar Lihui Yang puts it, "China boasts abundant myths about culture heroes and their inventions. These inventions refer to the ordering of human life; acquisition of a livable environment; acquisition of a food supply for humans; creation of crafts, arts, and wisdom; establishment of customs and laws; and so on."[6]

Another reason that ancient Chinese religion and the myths connected to it are different from those of other ancient peoples is that China has an unusually large number of creation tales. Moreover, many of them completely contradict the others. This is in marked contrast to Judaism, Christianity, and Islam, which feature a single, clear-cut creation story. In it, God fashions the earth and says there should be light, and light immediately appears.

By comparison, some of the multiple Chinese creation myths do not even tell where the gods and culture heroes came from.

Instead, those deities already exist when the creation of the world itself begins. Moreover, of those Chinese creation tales that *do* tell how the gods came to be, Yang explains, "Gods and heroes may be born by a divine father and mother; come from an egg or other object; be created from air or sound; come from another god's corpse; be made by other deities with mud; or may be transformed from a monkey."[7]

Pangu and the Cosmic Egg

Since describing all the diverse Chinese creation stories in detail would by itself fill an entire book, most modern myth tellers concentrate on the handful of the most popular ones. Regarding those, by far the most often repeated tale is the one involving the appearance of the very first god—Pangu. The Chinese scholar Xu Zheng, who lived in the 200s CE, was the first person to record Pangu's story in writing. But modern experts think the myth itself was several centuries old by that time. Some suspect it arose among the residents of southern China; others think it may have been partly inspired by an ancient Hindu creation story popular in neighboring India.

PANGU
The first god, who emerged from the cosmic egg and created the heavens and earth

Whenever and wherever Pangu's tale originated, in it he created the universe that now exists and made possible the emergence of the other Chinese deities. This universe arose from a mostly dark and formless chaos that held within it a large egg.

In one version of this story, Pangu was already inside that cosmic egg, and no one knows, or will ever know, where he came from. In another version, the egg was at first empty, and Pangu suddenly appeared within it. All versions of the myth agree that he slept for eighteen thousand years and then awakened. During that long period, he had been maturing and growing, so at the moment he woke up and burst out of the egg, he was a towering giant. As for what he looked like, different

The creator god Pangu, seen here in an engraving, was said to have originated and grown larger within a special cosmic egg. When he eventually broke out of the eggshell, the story goes, he was enormous in size.

ancient Chinese writers offered diverse ideas. Some claimed he was naked and covered with hair like an animal; others said he wore a huge bearskin; and still others described him with a dog's head, a human head with horns protruding from it, or a human head without horns.

Whatever Pangu looked like, he was upset that he was surrounded by nothingness and chaos and became determined to bring order to it all. First he imagined an ax in his mind, and instantly an ax formed in his hand. With that tool he chopped up the remnants of the cosmic egg, whose lighter parts floated up to become the sky. Meanwhile, the heavier elements sank downward and became earth's solid surface.

This bringing of order to disorder was not a quick process. In fact, it took another eighteen thousand years. At the end of that period, Pangu was satisfied, but he was also quite exhausted. So he lay down to rest, and soon he died. Even in death, however, that mighty first god was not finished creating. As University of Oxford scholar Tao Tao Liu Sanders tells it:

> His body changed to create the world as we now know it. His last breaths turned into wind and clouds, his voice turned into thunder, his left eye turned into the sun and his right eye into the moon. His body and limbs turned into mountain ranges and his blood became flowing rivers. Every part of his anatomy became part of nature. The hairs on his body turned into trees and flowers, the parasites living on his skin turned into animals and fishes and his bones formed different kinds of precious stones and minerals. Even his sweat turned into dew.[8]

The Fashioning of Humans

While Pangu's body was steadily transfiguring into the many and diverse aspects of the natural world, high above in the heavens that he had earlier fashioned, a different sort of creation was at work. In ways that no one has yet explained, in the midst of the sky various other gods and spirits sprang into being. They looked down on the earth's surface and marveled at Pangu's magnificent act of creation.

One of those newer deities, however, felt that something was missing. Her name was Nuwa. Various ancient ac-

NUWA
One of the so-called Three Divine Sovereigns and the creator of the human race

26

Did Pangu Have Helpers?

Literally dozens of ancient versions of the tale of Pangu's creation of the world have survived. Although they all have similarities, most differ considerably on the details of that first god's accomplishments. For example, while a majority of the accounts say he acted alone, a few claim he was aided by four mythical creatures. One was a giant turtle that lent its sturdy body to propping up parts of the sky while Pangu was working on earth's surface features. (Later, Nuwa used its legs to hold up the falling sky.) The second mythical beast that helped the creator god was a large white unicorn. It used its horn to bore holes in the ground, in which Pangu planted trees. The third mythical helper was a *qilin*. A gentle, beneficial dragon-like creature common to Asian mythologies, the *qilin*, like the dragon, was seen as a symbol of wisdom and innate, potent power. That is why many Chinese and other Asian rulers used its image on their crests and shields. The original *qilin* offered Pangu valuable advice on how to most effectively shape earth's environment. Pangu's fourth animal helper was a phoenix, a special bird that supposedly emerged from a pile of ashes. It flew across the infant earth and kept Pangu informed about the progress of creation.

counts say her body had two main and very different sections. Her upper torso was that of a well-proportioned woman, while her lower body looked like that of a scaly, claw-footed dragon.

What Nuwa felt was missing from earth's surface was a race of mortal beings (as opposed to the gods, who were immortal). In her mind, they would not only give the newly created world more purpose but also provide her with companions to talk and play with. For these reasons she took it upon herself to create that race, which she called humanity. Nuwa floated above earth, searched far and wide, and decided that China's Yellow River valley would be an ideal place for her creations to live. So she descended to that river's banks, which were thick with soil rich in nutrients of all kinds. Scooping up handfuls of the moist loam, she began molding them into human bodies.

Nuwa, the divine being who created humans, is seen in this early-twentieth-century illustration. Her head, and in some accounts her upper body, were humanlike and her lower body was serpentine or dragon-like.

At first the goddess made the humans one by one. But after a while she speeded up the process by rolling a tube of sugarcane in the mud. According to Sanders:

> As she flicked the cane out onto dry land, small drops of mud fell off and were instantly transformed into men and women. Later, some people used to say that those whom she shaped with her own hands were the fortunate and well-endowed people of the world, while those who were formed by the shaking of the length of cane were the poorer and less fortunate people. Eventually, having created enough men and women, Nuwa instituted marriage among them so that they could procreate and continue the human race without any further help from her.[9]

The Day the Sky Fell

Nuwa's monumental contributions to humanity and its well-being did not end there. A number of Chinese myths also tell how a few generations after she created the human race, she saved it from destruction. The trouble began when the fire god, Yan-di, grew angry at the water god Gong-gong. When the myths were written down many centuries later, no one could remember why Yan-di was so annoyed and why he attacked Gong-gong, initiating a furious struggle.

The battle raged for a long time, and eventually Gong-gong lost. He was so angry with himself that he smashed his head against Mount Buzhou (a peak that exists only in the ancient myths). Because that mountain was one of the key pillars Pangu had erected to hold up the sky, parts of the heavens began to sag and fall down onto earth's surface. For months, earthquakes made the ground heave, forest fires spread far and wide, and huge sea waves rushed inland, drowning large numbers of people and animals. Misery seized hold of people everywhere, and it appeared that humans might soon become extinct.

Seeing what was happening, Nuwa felt compelled to aid the beings she had so lovingly created. Swooping down to earth, she found the remains of a giant turtle that had recently died. Thinking quickly, she cut off its legs and used them to prop up the sections of the sky that were sagging. Noticing that the badly damaged sky still had several gaps, she gathered many tons of colored stones, melted them down into a thick, sticky liquid, and used it to patch the gaps. Thanks to these heroic efforts, humanity averted destruction, making succeeding generations of people possible.

The Three Divine Sovereigns

Due to her fantastic feats in service to humans, later ancient Chinese writers honored Nuwa by naming her as one of the Three Divine Sovereigns. The other two were Fuxi (pronounced FOO-shee) and Shen-nong. They are sometimes also called the Three

Sage Rulers or the Three August Ones. In addition to creating humanity and saving its members from destruction, the three sovereigns were said to have introduced numerous crucial aspects of Chinese culture, including medicine, agriculture, writing, and music. Each also supposedly ruled China in the distant past, long before the first human dynasty took charge.

In this painting Nuwa appears with her brother (or in some accounts her husband), Fuxi. Some myths claimed that Fuxi was a kindly, caring individual who taught humans how to fish, hunt game, and raise livestock.

Depending on which myth one looks at, Fuxi was variously Nuwa's brother, mate, or close friend and ally. Like her, he was said to have a human's upper body and the lower body of a dragon. Legends claim that Fuxi taught people how to hunt and fish and raise domestic animals. In one of his most popular myths, after he showed humans how to fish, the ruler of the ocean at the time—the Dragon King—became angry. That being worried that if people started doing a lot of fishing, his own subjects—the fish—would all be consumed. Eventually, when he saw that his fish easily replenished themselves in the wake of human fishers, he no longer saw fishing as a threat.

Fuxi introduced many other cultural innovations as well. For example, he established the so-called marriage rule of ancient China. That statute, Yang writes,

> required a young man to give his fiancée two deer skins as an engagement gift. He made some musical instruments, such as the *se* (a twenty-five-stringed plucked instrument), and the *xun* (an egg-shaped clay wind instrument with finger holes). . . . [He also] raised livestock and horses to draw carts and carry heavy goods. He smelted metal and made numerous material objects and tools. He taught people to barbecue food and to pound grain with a mortar and pestle. Fuxi also made cloth and began to rear silkworms. He made coins of copper. He invented written characters for people to record life [and] also invented the calendar and laws.[10]

The third sovereign, Shen-nong, which means "Spirit Farmer" in Chinese, introduced agriculture and made the first plow. He also created the first marketplaces, in which people bought and sold food, cloth, and other goods. In addition, Shen-nong closely observed the plant kingdom, especially herbs, and showed how certain herbs could be used for medical purposes.

The Five August Emperors

The ancient Chinese credited a number of other aspects of the creation of culture to five mythical rulers collectively known as the Five August Emperors. The first, Huang-di, also called the Yellow Emperor, supposedly ruled all of China from 2697 to 2597 BCE. (Most ancient Chinese did not know the actual dates for the country's earliest rulers and dynasties, so they did not realize that no major kingdom ruled by an emperor existed that far back. Thus, they assumed that Huang-di and the other Five August Emperors had been real rulers.)

In his myths, Huang-di was described as both an ideal ruler and a highly creative individual. Among his supposed major cultural achievements was the development of astronomy and mathematics. Legend claimed that he also developed scales of notes for musicians and invented new measuring instruments for architects and builders. In addition, Huang-di was said to have sponsored court physicians who made strides in diagnosing disease.

> **ZHUANXU**
> The second of the Five August Emperors; legends claim he instituted important religious reforms

The second mythical culture hero in the group, Zhuanxu, supposedly reigned from 2514 to 2436 BCE. The grandson of Huang-di, Zhuanxu instituted a number of religious reforms, including making a deal with the gods. Before his reign they came to earth often and freely socialized with selected humans. Zhuanxu persuaded them to visit earth only when it was absolutely necessary.

The third august emperor, Ku, who was Zhuanxu's nephew, was thought to have ruled from 2436 to 2366 BCE. According to his myths, he dearly loved music and requested that many talented composers create new musical works that later became renowned in China. He also invented several new musical instruments.

Ku's son, Yao, was the fourth of the five inventive emperors. Reigning from 2358 to 2258 BCE (according to legend), Yao was a born politician and managed to unite many of the Chinese clans, large groups of families related by blood. Before his reign, the clans had often fought one another, but Yao brought peace to China, which saved lives and increased prosperity.

Yao also handpicked and trained his successor, an equally astute politician-statesman named Shun, who became the fifth of the august emperors and reigned from 2258 to 2195 BCE. Shun expanded and protected China's growing cultural advances by urging as many common people as possible to take advantage of those advances. There were a number of primitive hunter-gatherers and crude farmers

China's Fragmentary Myth Tellers

Ancient China had no writers, poets, or myth tellers who were equivalent to the ancient Greek epic poets Homer and Hesiod and the ancient Roman writer Ovid. They penned long, detailed compilations of traditional Greek myths and thereby preserved those tales in an orderly and fulsome way for future generations. In early China, in contrast, although a number of writers did record myths, they did so in a fragmentary, hit-and-miss manner. Most often they produced works about history or philosophy. Here and there within those texts, the authors mentioned or retold part of an old myth in order to illustrate a point they had just made. Only in modern times did scholars sift through those ancient documents, isolate the fragments of myths they contained, and collate and organize them into collections of complete legendary tales. The fragmentary approach taken by the ancient Chinese writers also partly explains why there are so many different versions of most Chinese myths. "These mythic fragments incorporated into miscellaneous [texts]," scholar Anne Birrell points out, "vary in their narration, and authors often adapted myths according to their own point of view." The result, she states, is that many old myths have three, four, or five versions—and some have more than a dozen.

Anne Birrell, *Chinese Myths*. Austin: University of Texas Press, 2000, pp. 13–14.

in the mountains and elsewhere who resisted, so Shun banished them to China's distant borderlands.

One of Shun's leading myths tells how he convinced most Chinese to share in the community spirit that he championed. When people in a given town or region were unhappy or troubled, the emperor disguised himself as one of the locals and worked alongside them for weeks or months. During that time, he used his forceful personality to convince them to be virtuous and work together with their neighbors to build a better society. Supposedly, each time he did this, the people in that area became far more peaceful and content.

By the time of Shun's passing, creation had run its grand course from Pangu to Nuwa down through untold numbers of centuries to the august emperors and Shun himself. Divine powers and inventive minds had both birthed and shaped Chinese civilization during those years. The foundation for China's incredibly long-lived and colorful subsequent history had been dutifully and lovingly laid.

CHAPTER THREE

Myths of Nature and Catastrophe

In addition to several creation stories, the earliest Chinese myths—dating from 1600 BCE or perhaps even earlier—were attempts to explain the wonders of nature. China occupies an enormous physical space and features many different kinds of geographical and geological features. These include vast river valleys, plains, forests, rugged mountain ranges, and an extensive ocean coastline in the east. The early Chinese wanted to know not only how all these natural wonders got there but also what caused natural processes such as rain, snow, thunder, lightning, storms, floods, earthquakes, and tsunamis.

As it was with most other ancient peoples, the general consensus with the Chinese was that the various facets of nature were the work of gods and other supernatural beings. Thus, the very ancient deity Chang'e oversaw the moon and its movements through the sky each month. Likewise, another early god, Yan-di, was in charge of the important natural phenomenon of fire. According to scholars O.B. Duane and N. Hutchinson:

> Compared to the other splendors of creation, the mountains and streams, the forests and flowers, humanity's importance is diminished. Never before, in any other culture

or early literature, was the emphasis on nature and humanity's communion with it so crucial. People's good fortune depended on their ability to behave in accordance with the dictates of heaven. From ancient times onwards, the highest ambition people could aspire to was to determine the natural law of things and to behave in sympathy with it.[11]

The Mighty Eight

Over time the Chinese added other diverse beings to the band of nature gods and provided each with one or more myths. Particularly crucial members of this group were the Ba Xian, or Eight Immortals. Like the Jade Emperor, they had once been real people, and their accomplishments were seen as so impressive that the government eventually deified them. Not only did they achieve many good deeds and perform miraculous feats, it was also thought that they knew nature's central secrets and that they could change the natural world in any ways they saw fit.

The first of the mighty eight, Li Tieguai, was the most famous of the lot. He was originally a human promoter of Taoism. According to his principal myth, he walked with a limp and used an iron crutch to steady himself. But that infirmity disappeared when he attained godly status. Before being deified, he accepted an invitation from the heavenly mother deity—Wang-mu—to visit her in her palace in the heavens. The goddess made it possible for Li's spirit to leave his body and journey beyond earth.

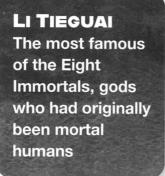

LI TIEGUAI
The most famous of the Eight Immortals, gods who had originally been mortal humans

Li asked one of his pupils to guard his body while his spirit form was away. After several days, the young student mistakenly thought that Li was dead and cremated the body. So when Li returned to earth, his spirit had no body to reenter. As a re-

A 1922 painting depicts the mythical Ba Xian crossing the ocean together. Better known in English as the Eight Immortals, they had once been human, but their achievements were so great that they came to be viewed as divine beings.

sult, he was forced to roam aimlessly from town to town. One day he came upon a lowly beggar who had recently passed away. Li entered the beggar's body and in it, now being in a sense one with nature, continued to travel. Soon he mastered the art of medicine by studying all the herbs in nature, and that allowed him to cure many people and even to raise a woman from the dead.

A Magical Soil-Like Sludge

At the height of the great flood that ancient myths claimed ravaged early China, the heroic dragon Yu saved humanity partly by creating dams and similar barriers of different sizes. To make these blockades, Yu utilized a substance called Xirang, which translates into English as "swelling earth." That mythical material, which appears in a number of ancient Chinese myths, was said to be a magical soil-like sludge that grew and expanded on its own, which made it perfect for repairing holes and gaps in walls and for building dams. Noted expert on Chinese mythology Anthony Christie tells how Yu used the swelling earth:

> Yu began his task by damming the springs from which the waters came. There were 233,559 of these, but with the swelling earth he could block them all. Then he built mountains at the corners of the earth to ensure that there would be regions that could not be submerged. They also served to anchor what was otherwise in danger of being swept away by the floods. Of course, there were inevitably small openings which escaped even Yu's thorough labors and it is because of these . . . that there are still floods today.

Anthony Christie, *Chinese Mythology*. Feltham, UK: Hamlyn, 1968, p. 88.

Another of the immortals, Zhang Guolao, was said to be blessed with powerful magical abilities. With them, he could subvert various laws of nature. For example, he was able to make his donkey paper thin, fold it up, and carry it in his pocket when not traveling.

The Age of the Ten Suns

The sun and its daily movements across the sky were among the diverse aspects of nature that the immortals at times bent to their will. One of the oldest Chinese nature myths of all describes how originally there were ten suns rather than simply one. They dwelled in a huge tree on the world's eastern edge. Each morning one of those suns climbed to the top of the tree and entered a chariot that took it across the great dome of the sky. Eventually, that sun reached another large tree on the world's western rim. And then, somehow, that sun managed to journey underground back to the eastern tree, where the cycle repeated with a different sun each succeeding day.

In another very ancient solar myth, one day all ten suns broke free of the eastern tree and floated into the sky. The heat they produced together was oppressive, and a terrible drought ravaged earth's surface. According to Duane and Hutchinson:

> Crops began to wilt, rivers began to dry up, food became scarce, and people began to suffer burns and wretched hunger pangs. They prayed for rains to drive away the suns, but none appeared. . . . They hid beneath the great trees of the forests for shade, but these were stripped of leaves and offered little or no protection. And now great hungry beasts of prey and dreaded monsters emerged from the wilderness and began to devour the human beings they encountered.[12]

Fortunately, the muscular archer god, Yi, saw what was happening. He saved the world by shooting down nine of the suns with special arrows that resisted their heat. The remaining sun, the myth concludes, was the one known to later ages, including the current era.

Tales of Thunder and Water

Just as the sun's history and movements were explained in myths, so too were natural occurrences such as thunder and lightning. Thunder, legends claim, was the work of a deity who was often called the Duke of Thunder. Named Lei-kung, artists depicted him as a grotesque, dark-skinned beast with a monkey's face and clawed feet. Despite his ugliness, he could be friendly and decent to others. In his best-known tale, for example, one day a young man was outside chopping wood when he heard thunder in the

Best known as the Duke of Thunder, Lei-kung had the face of a monkey and clawed feet. He was a friendly deity who sometimes helped people, as in the well-known myth in which he freed a young man from jail.

distance. The youth took shelter beneath a tree, and seconds later a bolt of lightning struck the tree. It began to fall, and as it did its branches snagged the Duke of Thunder as he was passing overhead. Trapped under the massive tree trunk, Lei-kung asked the young man to free him from his predicament, and the boy did so.

About a year later, the young man had a bit too much to drink one night and made enough noise to wake up his neighbors. The local constable soon arrived and carted the boy off to jail. While sitting in his cell, the prisoner prayed to Lei-kung and requested that the deity free him, just as the boy had freed the Duke of Thunder the year before. Sure enough, Lei-kung heard the boy's plea and rushed to the village. Letting loose his wrath, the god delivered a series of monstrous thunderclaps that shook the walls of every building in town. The terrified authorities immediately freed the young man, who till his dying day remained fast friends with the Duke of Thunder.

Among the many other nature deities the ancient Chinese recognized were several who controlled bodies of water. They included multiple sea gods, as well as supernatural beings who dwelled in and guarded lakes. Perhaps most important of all these water gods were those who controlled the rivers. This is because for the most part, China's earliest civilizations grew up along the banks of major rivers. Each river had its own local deity, but the most revered and influential river god was Ho Po, the lord of the Yellow River, China's most crucial waterway. Like most other river deities, in early times he demanded that human worshippers make offerings to him so that they would stay on his good side. Sometimes these offerings included human sacrifices, among them young women who would become the god's brides.

Ho Po
The deity who controlled the Yellow River

In one well-known myth, the officials of a major town on the Yellow River conducted their annual ceremony in which they prepared a young woman to become Ho Po's new wife. They dressed her in fine clothes and had a feast attended by the most respected townspeople. Finally, they placed the girl on an intricately decorated barge and set it adrift on the river. Ho Po then claimed his new bride.

Like One Vast Ocean

In real life, from time to time China's largest rivers flooded, in the process causing considerable destruction of property and loss of life. Such disasters were echoed in myths, especially the dramatic tale of a great flood that supposedly ravaged most of China in its earliest era. It was said that the flood took place during the reign of the well-meaning ruler Yao, the fourth of the Five August Emperors. Despite his strenuous efforts to bring order and harmony to his kingdom, many of his subjects became sinners and criminals.

Not surprisingly, the leading gods frowned on this situation and caused torrential rains to pour down on China. As one modern account describes it:

> Day after day the rains beat down upon the soil, pulverizing the crops that remained, flooding the houses, swelling the rivers to bursting point, until eventually the whole of the earth resembled one vast ocean. Those who were fortunate enough to avoid drowning floated on the treacherous waters in search of tall trees or high mountains where they might come to rest. But even if they managed to reach dry land, they were then forced to compete with the fiercest beasts of the earth for food, so that many were mercilessly devoured.[13]

Humanity's misery continued until a little-known deity named Gun expressed pity for the humans. He tried to stop the continually rising waters. But the fire god, Yan-di, saw what Gun was doing and attacked and killed him. Or at least it appeared that Gun was dead. The reality was that he was merely unconscious, and deep within his body a child was growing.

YU
The heroic dragon being who saved humanity from extinction in the great flood

That son, named Yu, ultimately burst forth into the light of day in the form of a powerful golden dragon. Determined to carry on his father's work of saving humanity, the magnificent creature constructed a vast dam of rocks and soil that held back the raging floodwaters.

The other gods saw what Yu had done and were so impressed with his

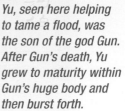

Yu, seen here helping to tame a flood, was the son of the god Gun. After Gun's death, Yu grew to maturity within Gun's huge body and then burst forth.

courage that they decided to let him go ahead with his efforts. When none of those deities intervened to stop him, he boldly flew up into the sky and dispersed the masses of moisture-bearing clouds. That rapidly halted the drenching rains, and soon patches of dry land began to appear. Within mere weeks nearly all of earth's dry lands were restored. Satisfied with this step, Yu now called upon his fellow deity, the Dragon King, Yinglong, and the two heroes spent many years repairing the terrible damage the great flood had wrought.

The myth of the great flood and the heroic dragon who saved the human race was beloved by the ancient Chinese, in part because it was dramatic and entertaining. But they also liked it because it contains motifs, or themes, that strongly resonated with them. In Anne Birrell's words,

> The flood introduces the theme of a return to primeval chaos. The myth of the hero is exemplified by Yu's great labors as he struggles to restore order. There are also the themes of a second beginning of the world, of human survival, and the restoration of human society to its dominant position over the animal kingdom. The most significant motif is that the flood is finally ended not by divine intervention, but through the agency of the moral hero, who puts his sense of public duty before private concerns and who performs his tasks with courage, obedience, and virtue.[14]

Man's Best Friend

Another important nature myth was the tale of the origins of the rice crops that filled China's natural habitat and for many centuries fed each new generation of Chinese. In a very real sense, this myth was a sequel to the story of the great flood. It also features a hero, although in this case it was not of the human variety. It was a dog.

The dog's story occurred a few years after Yu brought about the end of the great flood. The survivors of the disaster wanted to plant rice and other crops as they had in the past. But the floodwaters had destroyed all the plants, so there seemed to be nowhere to recover the seeds required to replant. As a result, people had to go back to the days when they relied principally on hunting animals to acquire food.

One day some hunters were out in a marsh looking for birds and other small game to kill or trap. Their faithful hunting dog was with them. The hunters did not realize that at the bottom of the marsh rested some seeds from rice plants and other crops that had been protected by some thick layers of mud and were still viable. Those seeds may have remained there in the mud and eventually become useless had it not been for a small flock of birds that flew by. The hunters let loose their arrows and struck two of the birds, which dropped down into the marsh.

The dog, whose task was to bring the dead birds back to the hunters, now went to work. It dove into the shallow water and grasped the feathered carcasses in her jaws. While it was scooping them up, its paws and tail dragged through the mud beneath, and a number of the plant seeds got stuck in its fur. When the dog returned to the hunters, they were far more interested in what was in its fur than what it carried in its mouth. They now had sufficient seeds to grow new rice and grain plants, and so nature's gift of agriculture was reborn.

The Tale of the Great Fire

Of the various ancient Chinese disaster myths, the one about the great flood is arguably the most famous. Another well-known tale of catastrophe was one that envisioned a tremendous fire that swept the world. It was one of several variations of the myth of the ten suns. In the most common version, when all ten suns entered the sky at the same time, a major drought ensued, destroying crops and forcing people to seek protection from the heat any way they could. In the myth of the great fire, that drought was only the first stage of the calamity. Eventually, the forests and houses caught fire, and the blazes raged for days or longer, until finally the archer god Yi intervened. In this version of the story, Yi went to a powerful sky god, Jun, and asked him how he could stop the fires. Jun gave the other deity a bright red bow with magical properties and some arrows made of a kind of silk that resisted flames. Only these, Jun explained, could wound the suns badly enough to cause them to fall into the sea. Yi thanked Jun, grasped the weapons, and hurried up into the sky. There, one by one he shot down nine of the marauding suns. After the fires burned themselves out and until the forests grew back, people rebuilt their houses using fieldstones and other materials that did not burn.

In an alternate version of the myth, popular in a different region of China, the dog managed to travel to heaven. There, it saw that some gods retained various seeds from earth plants. Realizing that humans needed those seeds to grow rice and wheat, the animal swiped the seeds and brought them back to its master's village.

To the Chinese, whichever of the two myths one accepted, it did more than tell how agriculture survived. It also explained why people have a compulsion to love and feed dogs. As Lihui Yang remarks, "Since the grains we have today were left on the earth because of the dog, humans today should give part of their food to dogs."[15]

CHAPTER FOUR

China's Fabulous Legendary Dragons

Myths featuring dragons exist in the mythologies of cultures around the world. The ancient Greeks, Mesopotamians, Norse, Hindus, and Africans, along with the medieval Europeans, had stories in which dragons or dragon-like monsters threatened human communities. Usually, one or more human heroes fought and killed those frightening beasts.

The ancient Chinese also had dragon myths—a fairly large number of them, in fact. What made most Chinese dragons different from those in the mythologies of other lands was that Chinese dragons tended not to be destructive and objects of fear and loathing. Indeed, the archetype, or model, for the Chinese dragon (called a *long*) was a large, powerful, but benevolent creature that cared about people and often brought good fortune. The latter typically included benefits such as needed rains to irrigate crops, good harvests, and prosperity for individual families, communities, or even kingdoms. Dragons were so revered, respected, and special in ancient China that a number of dynastic emperors would not allow anyone but themselves to use images of dragons in family crests or coats of arms.

Regarding such images, China's dragons had certain physical characteristics and roles in nature that were consistent in

Chinese dragons, like the one pictured here, were often imposing but kind creatures. They were thought to bring good fortune.

almost all the country's dragon myths. According to Tao Tao Liu Sanders, a *long*

> breathed not fire, but clouds, and has been described [in ancient texts] as having the head of a camel, the horns of a stag, the eyes of a demon, the ears of a cow, the neck of a snake, the belly of a clam, the scales of a carp, the claws of an eagle, and the paws of a tiger. Very often,

however, he appeared in human form. His element was water and he controlled rainfall as well as the water in rivers, lakes, and streams. [Each] sea, river, or lake had its guardian dragon, often of kingly status, living in a crystal underwater palace surrounded by priceless treasures.[16]

That high societal status enjoyed by dragons was frequently reflected in the way the ancient Chinese compared specific people to those unique creatures. A high-achieving, popular, or unusually kind and helpful person was sometimes called a dragon. (Conversely, a low-achieving, unpopular person in ancient China might be called a worm or a slug.)

Sun and the Dragon Prince

Indeed, dragons were so respected in ancient China that they were often closely associated with emperors and other rulers. Moreover, in a few myths certain rulers were actually semidivine, immortal dragons who took human form while on the throne. This occurred in the popular story of the ancient healer Sun and his dealings with a family of royal dragons.

SUN
An ancient healer who saved the life of the Dragon King's son

Sun, who dwelled in the countryside, often spent long hours in the forest searching for herbs that he might convert into medicines to treat sick people. One day he rounded a bend in the path and beheld a shepherd using a stick to beat a small blue snake, which was desperately trying to avoid the blows. Filled with pity for the unfortunate creature, Sun offered to give the other man his warm cloak if he would stop attacking the snake. The shepherd agreed, took the cloak, and left. In the days that followed, Sun used a mixture of healing herbs to nurse the creature back to health, and it finally slithered away into the underbrush.

A week later Sun was again out collecting plants when four men mounted on horses rode up to him and asked his name.

Guo Pu the Myth Teller

One of ancient China's leading myth tellers was Guo Pu, a poet and historian who flourished in the late 200s and early 300s CE. A staunch Taoist, he felt that myths were valuable because they helped people learn about the gods and the moral examples those beings had supposedly set for humans. Hence, he spent much of his time commenting on and producing new versions of old mythological texts. In particular, he studied and thoroughly commented on *The Classic of Mountains and Seas*, a large collection of myths created sometime in the fourth century BCE. By the time Guo Pu studied that ancient text, its language was archaic and hard for average people to understand. So he often rewrote its stories to make them intelligible to people in his own time. In the process, he changed many of the details of those original myths (some of which were already altered versions of even earlier texts). Another of Guo Pu's distinctions was that he was a key founder and developer of feng shui, a Chinese pseudoscience that suggests that people can employ mystical energy sources to live harmoniously with nature. In fact, many people today call Guo Pu the "father" of feng shui.

When he identified himself, they asked him to accompany them to the nearby capital city of the kingdom in which Sun resided. There, they explained, the ruler—the well-known Dragon King—was anxious to meet the humble healer. Assenting to this request, Sun went with them and soon stood before the king in his majestic throne room. The ruler, a tall, handsome, bearded man, stood beside a boy who was in his early teens and wore a finely made blue outfit.

To Sun's surprise, the king, gesturing to the boy as he spoke, sincerely thanked the healer for saving his son's life. The king and prince, the monarch said, were dragons who could take the form of any animal, and the boy enjoyed transforming himself into a snake. If it had not been for Sun, the Dragon King pointed out, the prince would not have survived the shepherd's attack. As a token of his thanks, the king then presented Sun with thirty thick volumes of medical lore known only to the semidivine dragon folk.

Thrilled with the gift, Sun spent months reading and rereading the books and learned a great deal about medicines and healing. Among the things he learned was that some poisonous plants could be eaten with no ill effect when combined with certain herbs. For many years to come, he roamed the kingdom, healing thousands of sick people and gaining a reputation as one of the finest physicians China had ever produced.

When Sun finally died at the age of one hundred, the elders of his hometown planned to give him a splendid funeral. But when they entered his house to place his corpse in the coffin, a wondrous thing happened. Sun's body dissolved into thin air, leaving behind only his robes. All those present realized that the dragon deities had lifted him up into heaven and granted him immortality.

The Astonishing Patch of Grass

The story of Sun and the prince contains notable magical elements, which is typical of most ancient Chinese dragon myths. Indeed, magic plays a very big role in one of the three most famous of those tales—the one that explains the source of dragons' wisdom, power, and immortality. Long ago, not far from the Min River (in south-central China), the story goes, a woman and her teenaged son dwelled in a lowly, one-room hut. Among the poorest people in their village, they managed to barely get by thanks to the son's relentless hard work. Each day, he went into the countryside and cut patches of tall grass, packed the cut grass in cloth sacks, and sold them to his neighbors, who used the grass to feed their livestock.

MIN RIVER GUARDIAN
A huge dragon, it was originally a human boy who underwent a major physical transformation

When the boy was sixteen, an awful drought occurred, and most of the tall grass in the area turned brown and died. As a result, he found it increasingly difficult to find enough usable grass, which meant he earned less and less money. After six weeks with no rain at all, the young man and his mother were literally sick from hunger.

Yet the boy refused to give up. He went out into the country-side one more time in hopes of finding some grass that was viable enough to sell. To his utter surprise, he came upon a large and incredibly lush patch of green, healthy grass. Astounded and de-lighted, he swiftly cut down the entire patch, bagged it, and sold it for a hefty profit. He and his mother could finally afford to buy enough food to last them more than a week.

The next day, the young man returned to the area where he had found the healthy grass. Again, he was astonished. Not only did he find more healthy grass, he discovered that it had grown up overnight in the very same patch he had cleared the day be-fore. Ignoring the fact that such a thing seemed impossible, the boy cut down the grass and sold it, making another large lump sum. This same amazing thing transpired on each of the five suc-ceeding days.

A Fantastic Transformation

At that point, the boy decided to save himself the long walks to the miraculous patch of grass by uprooting it and replanting it next to his hut. While digging out the roots, he came upon a mag-nificent rose-colored pearl. At first, he and his mother planned to travel to the nearest city and sell the object in the marketplace. But that night they found that size and beauty were not the pearl's chief values. When they placed it in a jar that also contained a single grain of rice, the next morning the jar holding the pearl was jam-packed with rice. As Sanders tells it:

> Realizing this was a magic pearl, they agreed to keep the knowledge to themselves and to put the pearl to good use. That night they put the pearl in the box where they kept their money and, sure enough, next morning the box was overflowing with coins. Then they tried the bottle

where they kept their lamp oil, and next day it was full of the best-quality oil. Using the pearl carefully, the mother and son became quite wealthy, and the boy did not have to go out cutting grass again.[17]

The neighbors naturally noticed this considerable change of fortune and most were happy for the mother and son. Two selfish, greedy villagers became suspicious, however. They went to the mother and boy and intimidated them into revealing the secret of their good fortune. When the two men announced they were going to take the pearl for themselves, the boy quickly popped it into his mouth and swallowed it. Immediately, the young man complained that he was extremely thirsty. No matter how many cups of water and tea his mother brought him, he wanted more, and before long he drank the nearby river dry.

In one famous dragon myth, a little boy swallows a pearl and then grows into an enormous dragon.

As the mother and the other villagers watched in amazement, the boy now underwent a fantastic transformation. In the words of O.B. Duane and N. Hutchinson:

> Horns sprouted on his forehead, scales appeared in place of his skin, and his eyes grew wider, and seemed to spit fire. Racked by convulsions, the boy grew bigger and bigger. The horrified mother saw that he was turning into a dragon before her very eyes and understood that the pearl must have belonged to the guardian dragon of the river. For every water dragon has a magic pearl that is his most treasured possession.[18]

When the boy had completely transformed into a dragon, he made it rain, and the river and nearby streams and lakes were brimming with water within a day. Sadly yet proudly, the mother wished her son well, knowing he would spend countless centuries guarding the Min River. Moreover, that marvelous caretaker was thereafter careful to keep safe his magic pearl, the source of his spiritual energy and remarkable powers.

The Four Dragons

Crippling drought was a central theme in another widely renowned Chinese dragon myth, most often called "The Four Dragons." The legend claims that in the country's dim past, before any rivers existed, humans and animals relied on rain only for water. This proved workable until a major drought occurred. For close to a year, it never rained at all, and thousands of people and animals died of starvation and thirst.

Seeing this devastation, four friendly dragons—by name the Long Dragon, the Yellow Dragon, the Black Dragon, and the Pearl Dragon—were sorely trou-

YELLOW DRAGON
One of the so-called Four Dragons and the creator of the Yellow River

The Nine Ancient Dragon Types

Several ancient Chinese myths claim that there were nine different kinds of dragons and that some looked distinctly different from the others. Also, each had its own likes and dislikes. So ancient Chinese architects and builders used the images of the separate dragon types in varying ways in architectural decorations. One of these types, called Bixi, was supposedly turtle shaped and adept at carrying heavy loads, so he was often pictured in sculptures on the foundations of stone monuments. The second kind of dragon—called Chiwen—was able to see long distances. His image frequently decorated the beams that held up the roofs of various large structures. The third dragon type, Taotie, enjoyed drinking large amounts of water, so his image was often sculpted onto bridges to ward off floods. The fourth type—Yazi—liked to get into fights; thus, his image was used to decorate sword handles. The dragon type Bi'an hated criminals; hence, his image embellished the gates of prisons. Another kind of dragon—Suanni—was said to enjoy being around fire and smoke, so its image appeared on Buddhist incense burners. The dragon type Baxia loved being in water, so its image was employed on the guardrails of bridges. Still another type of dragon, the Jiaotu, did not like guests entering its house; thus, its image appeared on the gates of houses. The last dragon type, called Pulao, loved music, so his image was used on bells and musical instruments.

bled. Hoping to help end the calamity, they obtained an audience with the leading god—the Jade Emperor—in his splendid heavenly palace. The dragons pleaded with him to step in and end the terrible drought that threatened to destroy humanity.

The Jade Emperor agreed to send plenty of rain, which would halt the drought. But not long after the dragons left his throne room, some palace officials approached him about some urgent repairs needed on that structure. Giving the matter his full attention, he forgot about his promise to make it rain on earth.

When ten days had passed and no rain had appeared, the four frustrated dragons decided that they must take care of the problem themselves. Flying out to sea, each used its enormous body to scoop up huge amounts of water. Then the powerful creatures flew across earth's surface, raining down life-giving water. Greatly relieved, thousands of people prayed and gave thanks to the Jade Emperor, thinking he had ordered the dragons to bring the rains.

One individual was not so happy, however—a sea deity who felt that the dragons had taken too much water from the ocean. That god complained to the Jade Emperor, who expressed displeasure that the four dragons had acted behind his back. As a punishment, he locked each dragon inside a mountain cave. This plan quickly backfired. Being water creatures with potent magic powers, the mighty beasts called forth torrents of water from deep underground. In this way, the Yellow Dragon made the Yellow River, the Long Dragon created the Yangtze River, the Black Dragon generated the Black River, and the Pearl Dragon fashioned the Pearl River. Thanks to the appearance of these permanent and plentiful water sources, the dragons happily realized, no drought, no matter how severe, would ever entirely wipe out humanity.

The Gigantic Candle Dragon

Not only did some dragons save humanity, as the famous Four Dragons did, a few particularly large dragons were said to affect humans' daily lives by controlling certain key aspects of nature. The best-known myths of this sort describe the gigantic Candle Dragon. It was said to live far to the north of China inside a mysterious legendary peak known as Mount Zhangwei. Perhaps the biggest dragon that ever lived, it supposedly measured more than 1,000 li in length. (Because 1 li was 500 meters, or a bit less than a third of a mile, the beast was about 300 miles long.

The Candle Dragon had a human head and face, while its crimson-red body had the form of a serpent. One of its eyes was the sun's brilliant disk, and the other eye was the moon's pale-white orb. Using its unique

THE CANDLE DRAGON

A mighty creature said to control the change from day to night and vice versa

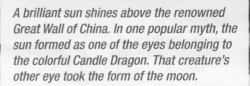

A brilliant sun shines above the renowned Great Wall of China. In one popular myth, the sun formed as one of the eyes belonging to the colorful Candle Dragon. That creature's other eye took the form of the moon.

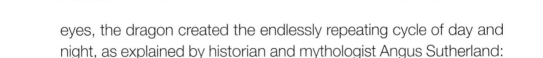

eyes, the dragon created the endlessly repeating cycle of day and night, as explained by historian and mythologist Angus Sutherland:

> The sun went down and darkness fell when he closed his eyes and when he opened them, the world turned into daytime. The Candle Dragon was mighty; he neither ate nor drank nor slept. He winked and winked, and days and nights occurred alternately. His breath produced strong winds and terrible torrential rains; once he blew, there would be winter in a second with the sky filled with black clouds and heavy snow storms; once he sniffed, there would be midsummer in no time with scorching sun that could even melt the stones.[19]

These mythical abilities of the immense Candle Dragon, when combined with the numerous other engaging tales of powerful, often heroic dragons, confirm Sanders's assertion that by far "the dragon is the most striking beast in Chinese mythology."[20]

CHAPTER FIVE

The Chinese Myths in Modern Culture

The large number of myths the Chinese compiled over the course of some two millennia were eagerly passed from generation to generation, and virtually every person was familiar with at least the major ones. These stories therefore could not help but have an influence on modern Chinese society. As Lihui Yang points out, "Those myths that have been handed down for thousands of years and contain Chinese people's philosophy, art, beliefs, customs, and value systems also have a great influence on Chinese society and culture."[21] Anne Birrell agrees, saying, "Although in one sense a mythic narrative becomes fixed once it is written down, it remains a flexible force in the sacred beliefs of a nation. The potency of ancient myth is expressed in many forms of Chinese culture—the arts, religion, state ritual, education, social mores, historical writing, in politics, and in the expression of national identity."[22]

Regional Religious Festivals

Birrell's mention of religion is important when examining the effects of the myths on modern society. This is because religion is mainly about worshipping the gods, and those deities who densely populate most of the myths are the very same deities worshipped in villages across China today. (China's Communist government officially advocates atheism. However, the country's constitution allows a few religious groups to worship freely as long as they do not disrupt public order or interfere with the state educational system.)

A prominent example of such worship is the Nuwa Palace Festival, held annually in March in She County (in northern China) to celebrate Nuwa, the goddess who created humanity. During the celebration, which attracts thousands of people, participants feast, pray, and listen to recitations of Nuwa's ancient myths. They also hear speakers recite and discuss newer Nuwa myths, including one conceived in the early twentieth century. In that tale, which takes place in the 1940s during World War II, an important Communist Chinese leader was hunted by Japanese invaders. Supposedly, Nuwa created a dense fog in which the leader successfully hid from his pursuers. Yang writes, "Such legends illustrate belief in Nuwa's protection and provide strong support for the preservation and transmission of her myths."[23]

A similar festival honors a deity named Hei-di Garnu, a goddess said to oversee population growth and the health of livestock. It is held every July 25 in parts of Yunnan Province, in south-central China. On that day worshippers pray to her and offer her gifts of food and drink.

One of the most famous and entertaining of China's annual celebrations of mythical characters is the Duanwu Festival, or Dragon Boat Race. It is held each year on May 5 in the river and lake regions of southern China. Often neighboring towns compete, and sometimes teams from an entire province take part. The boats, which come in all sizes, are shaped like various types of dragons from the old myths.

The Chinese seem to have a myth to explain practically every custom, and the popular boat race is no exception. Legend claims that the widely admired poet Qu Yuan, who lived during the Warring

QU YUAN
An ancient Chinese poet remembered in a tale in which he dies a tragic death

China's Duanwu Festival, centered on the Dragon Boat Race, is based on old Chinese myths. Each year, teams of racers take part in the celebrations.

States period (ca. 475–221 BCE), became deeply depressed for reasons that scholars still debate. In despair, the story goes, he waded out into the Miluo River and drowned himself. Some friends launched their boats and rowed at top speed, hoping to save him. But it was too late, and ever since, in his honor, people have held the renowned race.

When the Souls of the Dead Rise Up

Among the other annual celebrations of mythology in modern China, even more highly anticipated and certainly no less entertaining than the boat race is the celebration of Ghost Month. It takes place for about two weeks, beginning on the fifteenth day of a year's seventh lunar month, a date that can vary from year to year. This colorful, feast-and-music-filled, and frequently raucous, collection of festivities is based on a widely popular ancient myth. In it, the god of the underworld and afterlife—Yang-wang—schedules a kind of vacation. Once a year he essentially gives the scary beings who guard the underworld's borders some time off.

On that day, the story goes, the souls of deceased folk are able to leave the underworld and return to the world of the living. There they often visit family and friends, or they may simply roam the streets. Moreover, some of those ghosts are said to be angry with or jealous of the living, and as a result desire to frighten people or do various kinds of mischief.

The Halloween-like celebration consists of a wide range of customs and activities supposedly built around appeasing those unsettled spirits. For example, in a few places in China, local businesses close down for a day or more, although that custom, which used to be very widespread, is quickly disappearing. More often, people set up tables in the streets and cover them with

Li He the Myth Teller

Among China's ancient myth tellers, Li He was one of the most prolific and fondly remembered. He was born around 790 CE, when Europe was still languishing in its early, mostly culturally backward medieval period. In contrast, at the time China was flourishing culturally during the years of the Tang dynasty (ca. 618–906 CE). Little is known about Li He's personal life. Apparently, he suffered from various illnesses, which surviving sources do not directly name, and died young—likely in his mid-twenties.

In the short time span in which he was an active writer, he showed significant talent as a poet and often worked fragments of popular myths into his verses. Some evidence suggests that he always carried writing materials in a cloth or leather bag. When an idea came to him, he jotted it down, dropped it into the bag, and later expanded it into a complete poem. Among the various myths he mentioned, his favorite kinds were those involving ghosts, monsters, and other fantastic legendary beings. Among his more famous descriptions of the shadowy realm of the spirits of the dead are those in his poems "Qiu lai" and "Shen xian qu."

diverse meats and fruits, in hopes that these will appease the ghosts. It is also common to burn incense both inside and outside the home. In addition, based on the notion that the roaming souls of the dead are drawn to water, people use colored paper to make lanterns in the shape of lotus flowers. They toss these into rivers, and as the lanterns float downstream, they are thought to help the spirits find their way back to the underworld.

Ghost Month also features various sorts of entertainment. Both local neighborhoods and entire villages and towns stage nightly shows that include pop concerts and old-style Chinese operas. Conforming to the mythical basis for the festivities, these performances are not just for the living but also supposedly please the ghosts. Alongside the shows, people hold feasts containing gourmet versions of foods such as broiled chicken, grilled pork, rice and fruit, and a number of special pastries. It is customary for families to offer some of the food to the spirits.

In addition to these customs, a number of normal activities are traditionally discouraged during the Ghost Month celebrations.

A dramatic presentation entertains people during Ghost Month, one of modern China's favorite holidays. The festivities frequently include stage plays, pop concerts, opera performances, and feasts.

As explained by *South China Morning Post* reporter Mark Sharp, they include the following:

> Disturbing offerings left out for the spirits; don't sweep them up. Leaving clothes outside to dry. A ghost might try them on and leave behind its negative energy. Avoid swimming. The ghost of a drowned person might pull you under the water. Don't urinate on a tree, as it will offend the spirit living inside. Also, remember to stay away from the woods at night. Don't take photos at night in case you capture a spirit. Don't leave external doors open at night. It is an invitation for ghosts to enter. Don't get married; it won't be a happy ending.[24]

A Strong Love of Dogs

Another quaint aspect of local customs and daily life in modern China that has been shaped by ancient myths is the relationship between people and dogs. There are some sectors of the country in which people slaughter and eat dogs. But in several regions, that practice is both detested and forbidden. The Yao and She Chinese ethnic groups, for instance, revere dogs as much, or more, than American dog lovers do.

In part, this strong love of dogs in various parts of China is based on the popular myth of Panhu. As that tale tells it, there was a small ancient Chinese kingdom in which the queen developed a terrible earache that lasted for three years. The court doctors tried but failed to cure it. When the situation seemed hopeless, suddenly a golden worm crawled out of the queen's ear, and the earache abruptly stopped. She kept the worm in a small container for a while, and one day the creature

PANHU
A mythical character who began as a worm, transformed into a dog, and then partially changed into a human

Ancient Myths and the Chinese Spirit

Certain widespread Chinese social values are based directly on ancient myths. A clear example is the common belief that if society is faced with a threat of some kind, average people should not sit idly by and wait for help. They should take direct action against that impending event. This attitude comes from a deep admiration for certain mythical characters. High on that list are the heroic efforts of Gun and Yu to fight back against the rising waters in the myth of the great flood.

Another common societal value that comes from a mythical incident is the notion that people should be tough, unyielding, and always strive to succeed when faced with obstacles. This idea comes partially from the myth of Kuafu, an ancient giant who set out to race with and overtake the sun in its journey across the sky. Kuafu refused to give up, even though the sun's heat caused him to eventually die of overheating and thirst. Many Chinese still remember Kuafu as a tragic hero whose courageous spirit should be emulated.

transformed into a dog, which she named Panhu. That clearly intelligent canine instantly became the queen's loyal companion.

Months later a war broke out between the kingdom and a rival realm. All on his own, Panhu snuck off to the enemy king's palace, bit off that monarch's head, and brought the grisly trophy back to his mistress and her kingly husband. This act ended the war, and the local royals were extremely grateful to Panhu. They were greatly surprised when he began talking and explained that for a reward he wanted to marry their daughter—the princess. The king told him, "Surely you don't think that I could let you marry the princess. After all, you are only a dog." Panhu responded, "If that is all you are concerned about, please do as I ask. Place me beneath a golden bell."[25] After seven days and nights beneath the bell, Panhu explained, he would turn into a human male.

This plan worked well until the princess accidentally stopped the transformation on the sixth day. By that time, Panhu had the body of a man, but his head was still that of a dog. As it turned out, the princess fell in love with him anyway, and they were married. Thereafter, she wore furry hats and scarves when they were in public so that they would look more alike.

One modern moral of this myth is that the Yao Chinese believe that they are Panhu's direct descendants. Therefore, to them mistreating a dog is a terrible sin. Yang describes the punishment among the Yao in some regions for accidentally eating dog meat; that person, he says, "would be made to butcher a pig and take a bath in pig's blood, then offer the pig as a sacrifice to [a god]."[26]

Animated Films

Probably the most visible and universally popular aspects of modern Chinese life based on the culture's myths are artistic genres involving motion pictures. This category includes animated films of various kinds, television programs, and feature films shown in theaters. One of the best-known and most beloved examples was the 2003 TV cartoon show *The Legend of Nezha*, produced by China Central Television.

The Nezha program was what people in the United States and other Western nations call a superhero show. In Chinese mythology, Nezha was a boy who was born under miraculous circumstances, soon became a hero, died, and was later resurrected and became a grown-up hero. Both in his youth and adulthood,

KUAFU
A mythical giant who attempted to outrace the sun in its journey across the daytime sky

he always fought for righteous causes. In the animated television version, as a child Nezha was not initially heroic. Rather, he struggled hard to do the right thing and eventually learned to be a valiant fighter for good causes. The show depicted not only Nezha's adventures but also other heroic mythical characters and their exploits. "Their myths were changed," Yang points out, "for the purpose of propagating values and morals for today's Chinese children to learn and follow."[27]

As early as the 1950s, Chinese filmmakers also made full-length movies based on old myths. Some, like the successful

2008 film *The Archer and the Suns*, were animated in the tradition of Walt Disney's world-famous feature-length cartoons. The main character in *The Archer* is the divine hero Yi, from the classic myth in which he employs a special bow to shoot down nine of the ten suns that have created a catastrophic drought.

Another successful animated film inspired by China's ancient myths was *The Extreme Fox*, released in 2014. The plot follows an ancient Chinese scholar who seeks to end his hometown's cultural backwardness. While working with his fellow villagers, he accidentally meets with a fox spirit, and the two engage in a series of adventures that result in positive changes for both the scholar's career and his village's reputation. The film is only one of several modern full-length Chinese cartoons that have adapted old myths about magical fox spirits. Another notable example is *The Beautiful Female Fox* (2019).

Numerous Live-Action Films

Meanwhile, in the late twentieth and early twenty-first centuries, Chinese movie studios and producers turned out numerous live-action feature films based on characters and events from mythology. Among the more popular entries was *The Eight Hilarious Gods* (1993). A comic takeoff of the famous Eight Immortals, it presents those revered legendary characters in a tongue-in-cheek manner, as bumbling but lovable criminals.

TAO TIE
Monstrous creatures that appear in several Chinese myths, as well as in the spectacular 2016 film *The Great Wall*

Much more serious in tone, as well as far more expensive to produce, was the 2016 release *The Great Wall*. Directed by popular actor, screenwriter, and camera operator Zhang Yimou, the film combines action, adventure, and horror and boasts elaborate digital special effects. The latter bring to life legendary monsters called the Tao Tie, one of the "four evil creatures of the world" in ancient Chinese mythology. (The other

THE GREAT WALL

12/ 日 颠覆想象

Chinese film director and
actor Zhang Yimou greets
the press during the 2016
premiere of his movie, The
Great Wall, *which starred
American actor Matt Damon.
The story was based in part
on myths featuring scary
monsters called the Tao Tie.*

three are the Hundun, yellow winged creatures; the Qiongqi, a monstrous flesh-eating beast; and the Taowu, a monster that threatens to plunge society into disorder.)

In the movie, the hideous, rampaging Tao Tie live in a hive-like colony with an equally repellent queen. Every sixty years they attack China's capital to obtain enough food to sustain the colony, but they must breach the Great Wall, which, the movie suggests, was erected to keep them out. Some European mercenaries, among them a character played by noted American actor Matt Damon, visit China and become embroiled in helping the Chinese defend the wall against the vicious beasts. In his review of the movie, veteran film critic Simon Abrams said:

> The film's action set pieces [major action scenes] are not only thrillingly large-scale, but visually rapturous, despite a preponderance of computer-generated imagery. There

are a handful of well-choreographed and well-directed, Damon-centric action sequences. . . . Who could remain unmoved after watching a group of individuals dangle, thrust, and throw everything they've got at a legion of deranged-looking creatures?[28]

When it comes to mythical monsters, to most Chinese even the blood-curdling Tao Tie must take a second seat to the legendary Jiangshi. The Chinese version of the undead creatures called zombies in Western culture, the Jiangshi are by far China's favorite scary mythical creature. Indeed, these monsters are so entrenched in Chinese culture that from the 1950s to the present day the country created more than one hundred movies about them. (That number includes films of varying lengths made for TV programs, music videos, short cartoons, and video games.) The first notable example was *The Case of Walking Corpses* (1957), directed by Wong Tin Lam. Only a few of the many successful later contributions to the genre include *Zombie in a Haunted House* (1959), *The Haunted Cop Shop* (1987), *Mortuary Blues* (1990), *Bio-Zombie* (1998), *Rigor Mortis* (2013), and *Zombiology* (2017).

The Ongoing Importance of Myths

Whatever their subjects may be, modern films based on China's old myths are but one example of how those ancient stories shaped the social attitudes and cultural interests of every Chinese generation up to the present. The myths constitute "a traditional genre that was primarily created in the ancient past and have been transmitted for thousands of years," Yang remarks. Despite their great age, he adds, those stories have "deeply influenced people's ordinary lives throughout history. They often help to shape people's attitudes toward the world, provide evidence and reasons for their behaviors, and supply meanings and models for their current lives."[29] Therein lies the ongoing importance of myths in the lives of the modern Chinese.

SOURCE NOTES

Introduction: A Fascination with Spirits and Monsters
1. Sara Lynn Hua, "Five Chinese Ghosts That Are Absolutely Terrifying," *TutorMing China Expats & Culture Blog*, October 31, 2016. http://blog.tutorming.com.

Chapter One: The Ancient Chinese and Their Gods
2. Anne Birrell, *Chinese Myths*. Austin: University of Texas Press, 2000, p. 14.
3. Emily Mark, "Most Popular Gods and Goddesses of Ancient China," Ancient History Encyclopedia, 2016. www.ancient.eu.
4. Birrell, *Chinese Myths*, p. 28.
5. John Bowker, *World Religions: The Great Faiths Explored and Explained*. New York: DK, 1997, p. 92.

Chapter Two: Creation of the World, Humans, and Culture
6. Lihui Yang et al., *Handbook of Chinese Mythology*. New York: Oxford University Press, 2005, p. 69.
7. Yang et al., *Handbook of Chinese Mythology*, pp. 63–64.
8. Tao Tao Liu Sanders, *Dragons, Gods, and Spirits from Chinese Mythology*. New York: Peter Bedrick, 1994, pp. 13, 15.
9. Sanders, *Dragons, Gods, and Spirits from Chinese Mythology*, pp. 15–16.
10. Yang et al., *Handbook of Chinese Mythology*, p. 121.

Chapter Three: Myths of Nature and Catastrophe
11. O.B. Duane and N. Hutchinson, *Chinese Myths and Legends*. London: Brockhampton, 1998, p. 10.
12. Duane and Hutchinson, *Chinese Myths and Legends*, pp. 52–53.

13. Duane and Hutchinson, *Chinese Myths and Legends*, pp. 64, 66.
14. Birrell, *Chinese Myths*, p. 35.
15. Yang et al., *Handbook of Chinese Mythology*, p. 54.

Chapter Four: China's Fabulous Legendary Dragons
16. Sanders, *Dragons, Gods, and Spirits from Chinese Mythology*, p. 48.
17. Sanders, *Dragons, Gods, and Spirits from Chinese Mythology*, p. 59.
18. Duane and Hutchinson, *Chinese Myths and Legends*, p. 114.
19. Angus Sutherland, "Legend of the Candle Dragon That Could Lighten the Darkest Gate of Heaven," Ancient Pages, January 15, 2016. www.ancientpages.com.
20.Sanders, *Dragons, Gods, and Spirits from Chinese Mythology*, p. 48.

Chapter Five: The Chinese Myths in Modern Culture
21. Yang et al., *Handbook of Chinese Mythology*, pp. 48–49.
22. Birrell, *Chinese Myths*, p. 65.
23. Yang et al., *Handbook of Chinese Mythology*, p. 49.
24. Mark Sharp, "Hong Kong's Hungry Ghost Festival: All You Ever Wanted to Know," *South China Morning Post* (Hong Kong), August 27, 2015. www.scmp.com.
25. Quoted in Sanders, *Dragons, Gods, and Spirits from Chinese Mythology*, p. 39.
26. Yang et al., *Handbook of Chinese Mythology*, p. 53.
27. Yang et al., *Handbook of Chinese Mythology*, p. 52.
28. Simon Abrams, "*The Great Wall*," RogerEbert.com, February 17, 2017. www.rogerebert.com.
29. Yang et al., *Handbook of Chinese Mythology*, p. 52.

FOR FURTHER RESEARCH

Books

Matt Clayton, *Chinese Mythology*. Scotts Valley, CA: CreateSpace, 2018.

Tammy Gagne, *Chinese Gods, Heroes, and Mythology*. Minneapolis, MN: ABDO, 2019.

Frederick H. Martins, *The Chinese Fairy Book*. Sandhurst, Australia: Arbella, 2017.

Frederick H. Martins and Richard Wilhelm, *Chinese Fairy Tales and Legends*. Sydney, Australia: Bloomsbury China, 2019.

Aaron Shepard, *The Monkey King: A Superhero Tale of China*. Bellingham, WA: Skyhook, 2019.

Philip Wilkenson, *Chinese Myth: A Treasury of Legends, Art, and History*. London: Routledge, 2016.

Internet Sources

China Culture.org, "Chinese Myth of the Creation of the World and Mankind," 2019. http://en.chinaculture.org.

Ducksters, "Ancient China: Mythology," 2019. www.ducksters.com.

Ducksters, "Ancient China: Religion," 2019. www.ducksters.com.

Ellen Lloyd, "Legend of the Eight Immortals Who Know the Secrets of Nature," Ancient Pages, May 21, 2016. www.ancientpages.com.

Emily Mark, "Ghosts in Ancient China," Ancient History Encyclopedia, 2019. www.ancient.eu.

Qiu G. Su, "A Guide to Ghost Month in China," ThoughtCo, 2018. www.thoughtco.com.

Angus Sutherland, "Legend of the Candle Dragon That Could Lighten the Darkest Gate of Heaven," Ancient Pages, January 15, 2016. www.ancientpages.com.

Edward T.C. Werner, "Myths and Legends of China: Fox Legends," Internet Sacred Text Archive. www.sacred-texts.com.

Kuan L. Yong, "108 Chinese Mythological Gods and Characters to Know About," October 31, 2019. https://owlcation.com.

Websites

Ancient Chinese Stories, Fables, and Legends for Kids (https://china.mrdonn.org/stories.html). This entertaining site, geared for young readers, features dozens of links, each leading to a short rendition of a common ancient Chinese myth.

Awakening Ancient Dragons, World of Chinese (www.theworldofchinese.com/2017/05/awakening-ancient-dragons). Nicely illustrated, this site retells the myths of arguably the five most famous dragons in Chinese mythology.

The Gods of Chinese Mythology, God Checker (www.godchecker.com/chinese-mythology). Conceived by the late modern mythologist Chas Saunders, this informational site explains the best-known ancient Chinese gods in a well-designed, eye-catching format.

INDEX

PICTURE CREDITS

Classical historian and award-winning author Don Nardo has written numerous acclaimed volumes about ancient civilizations and peoples. They include more than a dozen overviews of the mythologies of the Sumerians, Babylonians, Egyptians, Greeks, Romans, Persians, Celts, and others. Nardo, who also composes and arranges orchestral music, lives with his wife, Christine, in Massachusetts.